My Mail

by Kathy Mormile
illustrated by George Ulrich

Scott Foresman

Editorial Offices: Glenview, Illinois • New York, New York
Sales Offices: Reading, Massachusetts • Duluth, Georgia
Glenview, Illinois • Carrollton, Texas • Menlo Park, California

I like to get mail. Each day I
check the mailbox. Most of the
time, I don't get any. But it is
fun to check anyway!

I like to send mail too.
I send notes to my friends.
Each note needs a stamp.
Without a stamp, the note
will come back to me.

Today I am sending notes to my
friends Kathy and Patty. They live
in a big city.

I take my notes to the mailbox.
It is only around the block. My
mom walks with me. I drop my
mail into the box.

We read the note on the
mailbox. There is only one more
pickup today. I think I will wait to
see where my notes will go next!

Mom and I tell funny jokes as
we wait. Soon a mail truck stops
right by the mailbox.

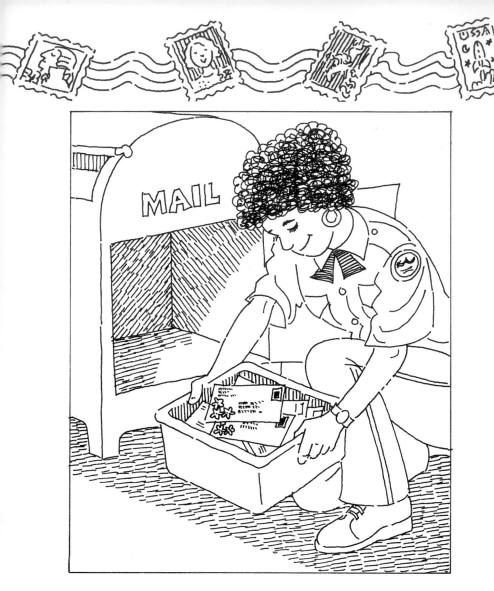

Sally gets out of the truck. She
looks in the mailbox. Then she
takes out a bin filled with mail.

Sally places the bin into the truck.
Mom and I watch as she places a
new bin inside the mailbox.

I walk over to Sally. I tell her
about my notes. I look in her truck.
There is so much mail!

Sally tells me all about the mail.
"When will my friends get their
notes?" I ask.
"Soon!" Sally tells me.
I wave good-by as Sally
drives away.

Sally was right. It didn't take
long. I heard from my friends.
They got their mail. They were
very happy!

Phonics for Families: This book provides practice reading words with long *e* spelled *y;* words with long *i* spelled *y;* compound words; and the high-frequency words *their, most,* and *heard.* Read the book together. Then have your child find all the story words that have long *e* and long *i* spelled *y.* You might also show your child a piece of mail that was delivered to your home. Point out the address, return address, and the cancelled stamp.

Phonics Skills: Vowel sounds of *y* (long *e*, long *i*); Compound words

High-Frequency Words: *their, most, heard*